COLOR YOUR OWN
MODERN ART
MASTERPIECES

Muncie Hendler

DOVER PUBLICATIONS, INC.
Mineola, New York

NOTE

Is it possible to create your own Picasso? Or an original Matisse? Yes, with this unique collection of 30 black-and-white line renderings of masterworks of modern art, art lovers and aspiring artists can experiment by altering the colors and hues of the original paintings and creating completely new paintings that reflect both the bold designs of their creators and the individual vision of the reader. How important are colors and tonal relationships to the meaning of modern painting? Change them and discover the answer for yourself. Color renditions of the original works are featured on the cover of this book if you want to reproduce the artist's colors.

Included here are the works of ten of the greatest modern painters, covering many of the major styles and movements of the twentieth century, including Abstract Expressionism, Fauvism and Cubism. Included are Fernand Léger's *The Big Parade,* Matisse's *Sorrows of the King,* Picasso's *Girl Before a Mirror* and *The Three Musicians,* Mondrian's *Broadway Boogie Woogie,* as well as works by Paul Klee, Joan Miró, Stuart Davis, Willi Baumeister, Atanasio Soldati and Auguste Herbin. The paintings are arranged alphabetically by artist and grouped for stylistic consistency. Captions identify the artist and the title of the work, the medium employed and the date of composition.

Bibliographical Note

Color Your Own Modern Art Masterpieces is a new work, first published by Dover Publications, Inc., in 1996.

DOVER *Pictorial Archive* SERIES

This book belongs to the Dover Pictorial Archive Series. You may use the designs and illustrations for graphics and crafts applications, free and without special permission, provided that you include no more than four in the same publication or project. (For permission for additional use, please write to: Permissions Department, Dover Publications, Inc., 31 East 2nd Street, Mineola, N.Y. 11501.)

However, republication or reproduction of any illustration by any other graphic service, whether it be in a book or in any other design resource, is strictly prohibited.

International Standard Book Number: 0-486-29328-9

Manufactured in the United States of America
Dover Publications, Inc., 31 East 2nd Street, Mineola, N.Y. 11501

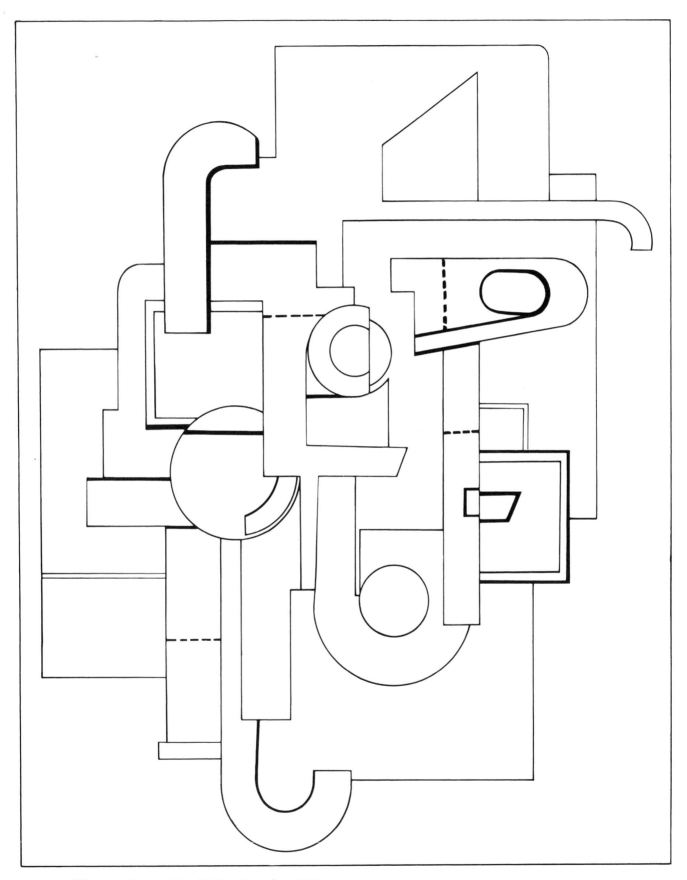

1.   **Willi Baumeister** (1889–1955). Gouache. 1923.

2.   Stuart Davis (1894–1964). Visa. Oil. 1951.

3.　**Auguste Herbin** (1882–1960). Vein. Oil. 1953.

4. Fernand Léger (1881–1955). The Big Black Divers. Oil. 1944.

5.   Fernand Léger (1881–1955). The Big Parade. Oil. 1954.

6. Fernand Léger (1881–1955). Leisure: Homage to Louis David. Oil. 1949.

7.   Fernand Léger (1881–1955). Man with Still Life. Oil. 1943.

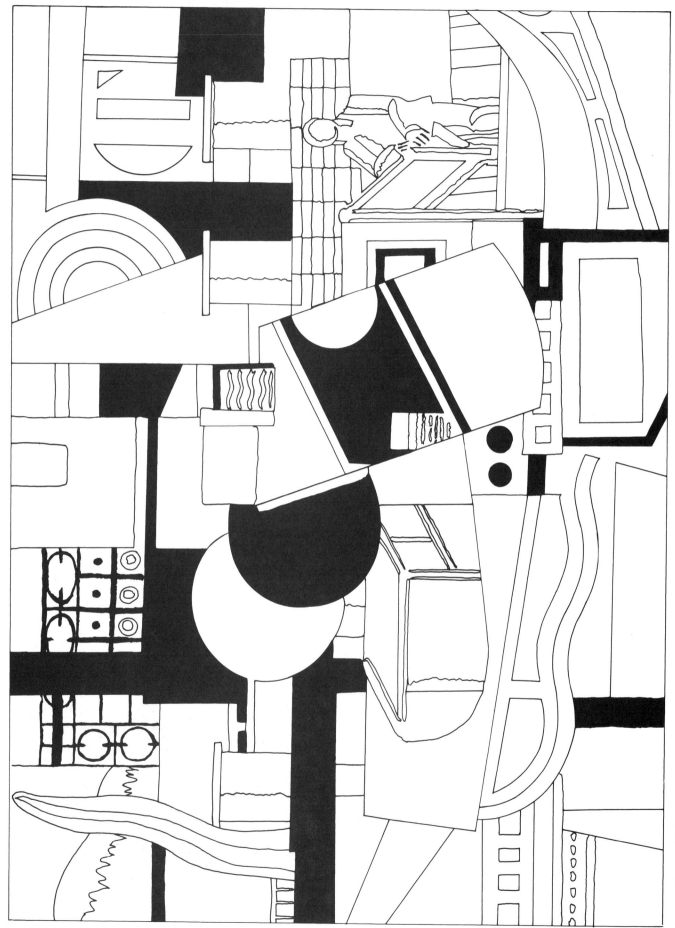

8.   Fernand Léger (1881–1955). The Deck of the Tugboat. Oil. 1920.

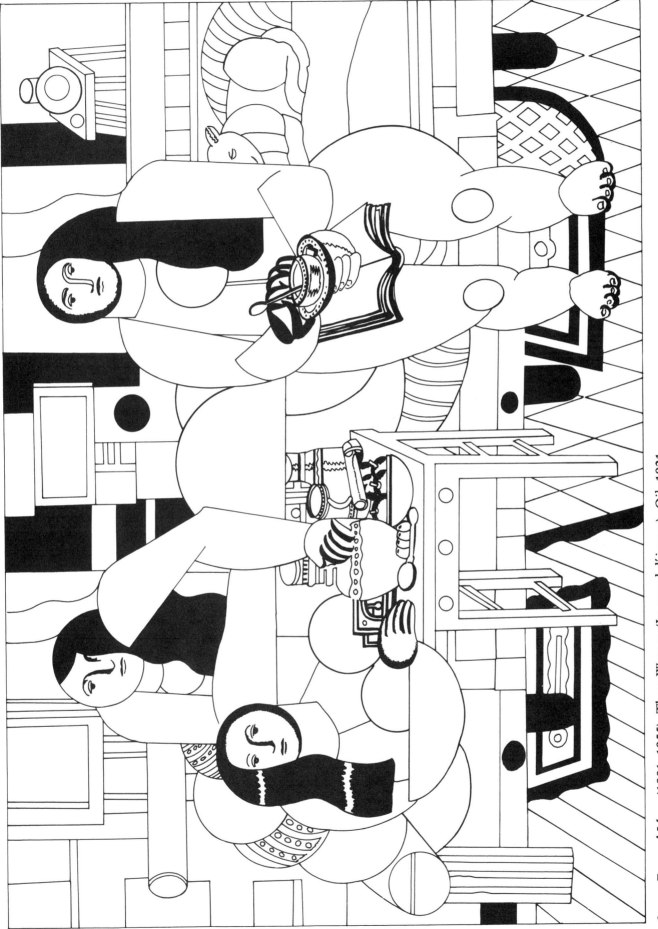

9.   Fernand Léger (1881–1955). Three Women (Le grand déjeuner). Oil. 1921.

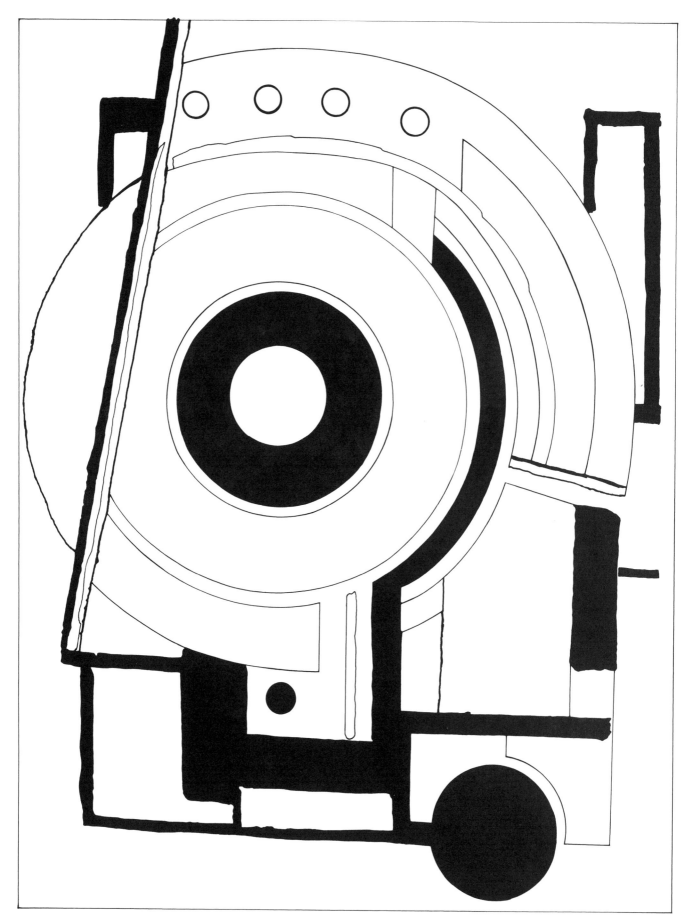

10.   **Fernand Léger** (1881–1955). Circular Composition. Oil. 1928.

11.   **Paul Klee** (1879–1940). Woman in Native Costume. Oil. 1940.

12.   **Paul Klee** (1879–1940). Clown. Oil. 1927.

13.   **Paul Klee** (1879–1940). Figure in a Garden. Oil. 1937.

14.   **Paul Klee** (1879–1940). Double. Oil. 1940.

15.   **Paul Klee** (1879–1940). Individualized Measurement of Strata. Oil. 1930.

16. **Paul Klee** (1879–1940). Stage Landscape. Oil. 1937.

17.   **Henri Matisse** (1869–1954). Sorrows of the King. Oil. 1952.

18.   Henri Matisse (1869–1954). The Piano Lesson. Oil. 1916.

19.   Joan Miró (1893–1983). The Swallow of Love. Oil. 1934.

20.   Joan Miró (1893–1983). The Harlequin's Carnival. Oil. 1925.

21.   Joan Miró (1893–1983). Snob Evening at the Princess's. Oil. 1944.

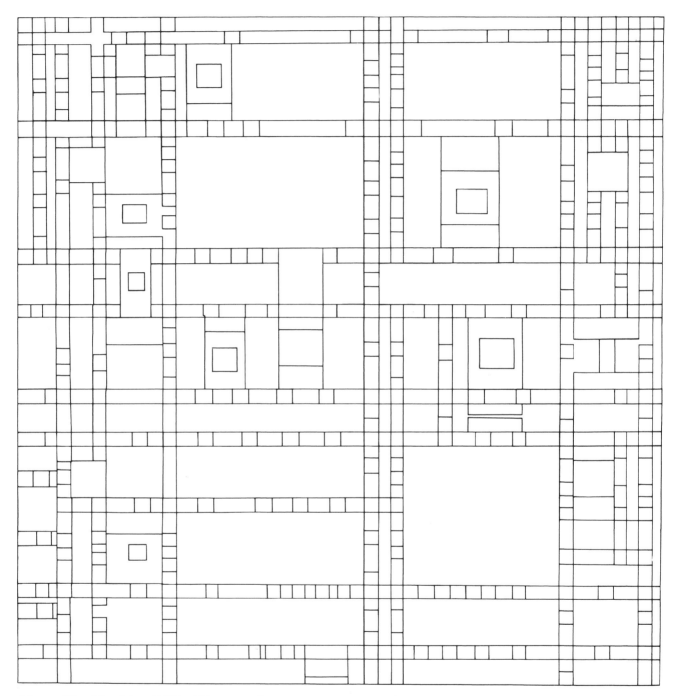

22.   **Piet Mondrian** (1872–1944). Broadway Boogie Woogie. Oil. 1943.

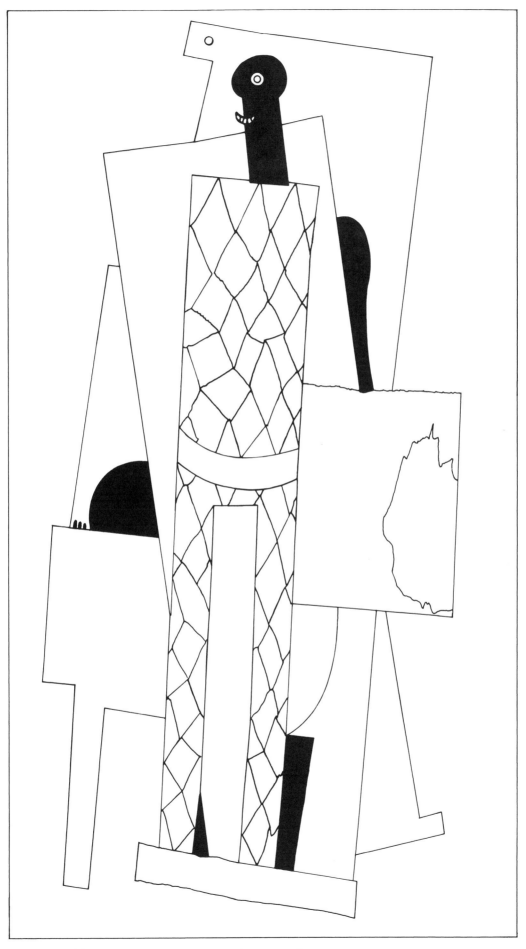

23.   **Pablo Picasso** (1881–1973). Harlequin. Oil. 1915.

24.   **Pablo Picasso (1881–1973). Three Musicians. Oil. 1921.**

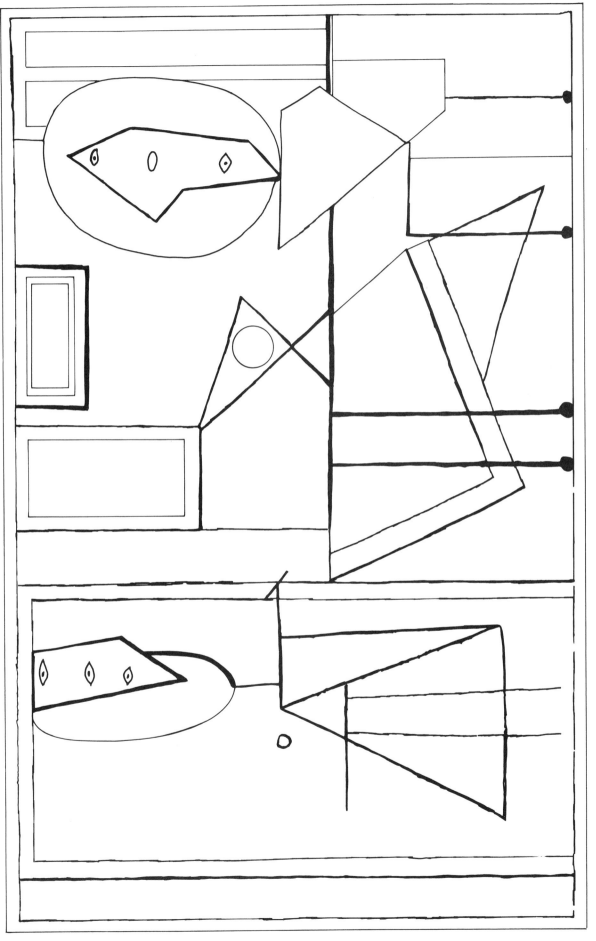

25.   **Pablo Picasso** (1881–1973). The Studio. Oil. 1928.

26. **Pablo Picasso** (1881–1973). Seated Woman with Star-Patterned Dress. Oil. 1939.

27.   **Pablo Picasso** (1881–1973). Jacqueline with Flowers. Oil. 1954.

28. **Pablo Picasso** (1881–1973). Girl Before a Mirror. Oil. 1932.

29.   **Pablo Picasso** (1881–1973). Woman with a Flower. Oil. 1932.

30. **Atanasio Soldati** (1896–1953). Composition. Oil. 1950.